UNDERSTANDING ENERGY

Martina E. Faulkner MSW

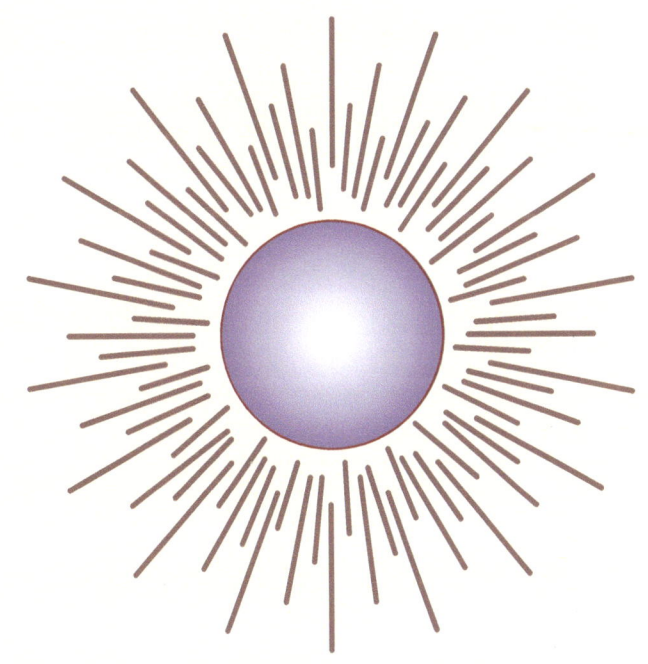

INSPIREBYTES OMNI MEDIA

Understanding Energy

This publication is published and distributed worldwide in the English language in the following formats:

ISBN Paperback: 978-1-953445-86-5
ISBN E-Book: 978-1-953445-87-2

This book was printed in a manner that minimizes its impact on the planet and the environment. Learn more at: www.inspirebytes.com/why-we-publish-differently/

 INSPIREBYTES OMNI MEDIA

Inspirebytes Omni Media LLC
PO Box 988
Wilmette, IL 60091

For more information, please visit www.inspirebytes.com
Graphics and photos: Canva Design Pro

"Love the moment and the energy of that
moment will spread beyond all boundaries."

– Corita Kent –

"What is this, that I have, that is not nothing?"

– William Shakespeare –

"Don't hold on to anger, hurt, or pain. They
steal your energy and keep you from love."

– Leo Buscaglia –

Contents

"Your energy introduces you even before you speak."

– Unknown –

Introduction

"Energy" is a word that gets used almost to excess in today's world. It represents a whole host of things from people's emotions to mysterious forces at work behind some sort of wizardly curtain. It's both tangible and intangible in how we apply it and understand it, which has opened it up to a lot of interpretation—and misinterpretation.

The truth is that energy is much simpler, cleaner, and more specific than our common usage of the word implies. As such, it also can become a bit more complex to understand when we strip away all the things it's not to land on what it actually is. That is because it's essentially a tangible intangible. Energy simply is, while also being something we can't really quantify. Not yet, at least.

So, what is energy? What does it do, or not do? How does it impact our lives? How can we impact it? And, perhaps more importantly, why does it matter that you understand all this?

Let's dive in!

What is Energy?

Energy is everything and nothing at exactly the same time. Everything is made up of energy. Literally, everything. The boulder sitting idle on the side of the road? The flower blooming at night? The bird flying overhead and the waterfall? They're all made up of energy. Similarly, you, your friends and family, your pets, and every stranger you meet is made up of energy.

Everything is energy.

Now, let's take it a step further. There are two kinds of energy... Yes, just two. At any given moment, all energy is either active or inactive. Energy that is active is called kinetic energy, whereas energy that is dormant is called potential energy. Everything you see—and even things you can't see—are always in one of these two states. When you understand the simplicity of this, it makes it easier to know how and when you can interact with energy.

To reiterate: Potential energy and kinetic energy are the two states of energy. This is why energy is everything and nothing. To learn how we can intentionally interact with energy, we turn to a famous line from Star Wars: "Use the force, Luke."

In that moment, Luke was invited to remember that everything around him is made of energy, and that he (also being made of energy) can tap into that level of being and move with it, interacting with everything around him.

So, in many ways, understanding energy is a way of actually developing a better understanding of our environment and the life around us—including how we interact with it. We all have an impact, whether we acknowledge it or not. Everything you do, will in some way affect everything around you. The impact does not have to be monumental to be felt or to move energy. In fact, it's often the subtle little things that can move energy the most.

For example, have you ever been in the presence of someone meditating? They aren't doing anything that you can see, just sitting there quietly, and yet their presence is directly impacting everything around them. Their "energy" is having an effect on all of the energy in their environment, and vice versa. Energy always is, therefore there is no way you can't be impacting your environment, from an energetic perspective. Nor is it possible for your environment to not be impacting you. From an energy perspective, there is no separateness.

As such, perhaps the most tangible way to explain energy is to see it as a means by which you can begin to understand your environment and your life in a more grounded, holistic, broader, and deeper capacity. Since energy is everywhere all the time—and you are made of energy—this perspective is what will actually help you to work with it in a more meaningful way.

Who Should Practice Energy?

> *"Energy is the currency of the universe. You get what you give."*
>
> *– Oprah –*

Throughout history, there have been energy workers, energy healers, and energy practitioners, in some form or another. Depending on the culture, religion, region of the world, and period of history, we have called them everything from: priests, priestesses, shamans, medicine women, medicine men, oracles, and so much more. Though their practices may be different, at their core, they're all the same... so take your pick. When it comes to understanding energy, all of these titles are essentially interchangeable.

Unfortunately, we have had so many different names for energy workers that the labels we have given them actually ended up creating divisions and hierarchies, which undermines the simplest truth about energy work:

Energy is a universal way in which we can understand the world around us better and interact and engage with it on a more holistic level.

At the end of the day, all the labels and names are a human construct and only serve to detract from the ultimate purpose of understanding energy. When you truly understand energy, you know its purpose is simple and completely devoid of any human value system.

Energy simply is.

> *"The way you think, the way you behave, the way you eat, can influence your life by 30 to 50 years."*
>
> — Deepak Chopra —

Working with energy is a tool we can use to achieve greater alignment, greater evolution, more growth, better well-being, better understanding, better connection, and all the things we hope for from a soul perspective. Idealistic? Perhaps, but no less true. If you take a moment to look at nature, when left alone, it works in harmony. Each aspect has a role and each role is carried out in balance with everything else. This is a perfect visual and tangible representation of energy.

When things are balanced and harmonious, that is energy at work in its most natural state, as both kinetic and potential energy.

So, who practices energy? (Or who should?)

At this point in our human timeline, there are many (many!) people practicing energy. We see energy practitioners working in different paradigms, using different practices and tools. Unfortunately, we also see numerous interpretations coming forward and being marketed as being "better" than anything that came before. This undermines the nature of energy by creating the aforementioned value-driven hierarchy.

To be clear, energy has no hierarchy. Is there one method or interpretation that is better than another? No.

> *"To heal is to touch with love*
> *that which we previously*
> *touched with fear."*
>
> *— Stephen Levine —*

There may be a practice or tradition that is better for you, but that does not mean it's better than any other modality of energy work. There is no "better" or "worse" when it comes to energy. Energy can't be pigeon-holed that way, because to do so limits it, and energy has no limits. Remember, it only has two states: kinetic or potential. It cannot be more or less than that.

This leads us to another simple truth about energy, and more specifically the practice of energy work, which is this: If someone says there is only one way to practice or engage with energy work, you should walk away. Because this is simply not true. When it comes to energy work, there are potentially millions of ways to engage in the work. The question should be: What is the best way for you to practice energy work? The answer will be based on your resources, your environment, and your personal values.

Though there are many different ways to practice energy work, just as there are even more energy practitioners in the world, there is still only one way to truly understand energy, which is that it is everything and nothing at the same time. It is active and inactive and it neither dies nor is created. Energy simply is, and nothing—and nobody—can change that.

> *"If you want to find the secret of the universe, think in terms of energy, frequency, and vibration."*
>
> — Nikola Tesla —

When Does Energy Matter?

Energy matters every day of your life, whether you practice it and/or understand it, or not. The simple reason for this is twofold: 1) everything is energy, so there's no escaping it or opting out, and 2) energy is a means by which you can understand life better. It's the second piece that makes energy matter the most, because when you understand that truth, you can create a cheat sheet to life and make it easier for yourself and others.

Energy is a way to understand—and interact with—your environment better. It's a filter you can use to help you engage with life differently—usually for the better. For example, many of us have experienced being at an event when a certain person walks in, and suddenly, the entire energy of the room is either lifted or dropped. Their presence directly impacted the energy of the room, just by showing up.

This is why understanding energy matters. How you show up in your daily life is entirely up to you and you are responsible for the energy you bring into a room.

Conversely, you are not responsible for anybody else's energy. In that instance, you are only responsible for how you interact with or react to somebody else's energy.

So, if you are the person who is bringing a room down (or lifting a room up), that is your responsibility. Nobody else is responsible for fixing or changing that for you.

Furthermore, they get to react in whatever way they wish to; that is their prerogative and responsibility. This is true every day of your life, for everything you do, everywhere you do it. Energy matters everywhere, all the time.

Understanding how you show up as energy may give you a greater sense of responsibility, but it can also give you a greater sense of empowerment. That empowerment can lead to stronger boundaries and a stronger presence, including where you are willing to put your attention. Focus is a form of energy.

When you focus on something, you are essentially saying, "This is where I want to put my energy." This includes:

- When and where you are willing to show up
- What you are willing to support
- Who you are willing to be around

All of these items are a choice that you get to make when you understand energy and accept that it matters... in everything.

"I do believe we're all connected. I do believe in positive energy. I do believe in the power of prayer. I do believe in putting good out into the world. And I believe in taking care of each other."

– Harvey Fierstein –

> *"Love is a sacred reserve of energy; it is like the blood of spiritual evolution."*
>
> — Pierre Teilhard de Chardin —

As you may now know, there are many different practices when it comes to energy work. There are even more people who teach these energy work practices, resulting in an increasing number of paradigms (or interpretations) of energy work practices. Remember: There is no "one way" or "one correct way" to study energy work. There is only what's best for you. This means it is incumbent upon you to do your due diligence when researching energy work practices and practitioners.

When doing your research, here are just a few of the questions you might want to ask:

- Where do they come from? What practice lineage?

- What do they believe? Personally and professionally?

- What have others said about them?

- Do they allow people to come and go from their practice?

- Do their teachings align with my values and beliefs?

- Can I afford this program? What are my resources?

- Do I feel any hesitancy?

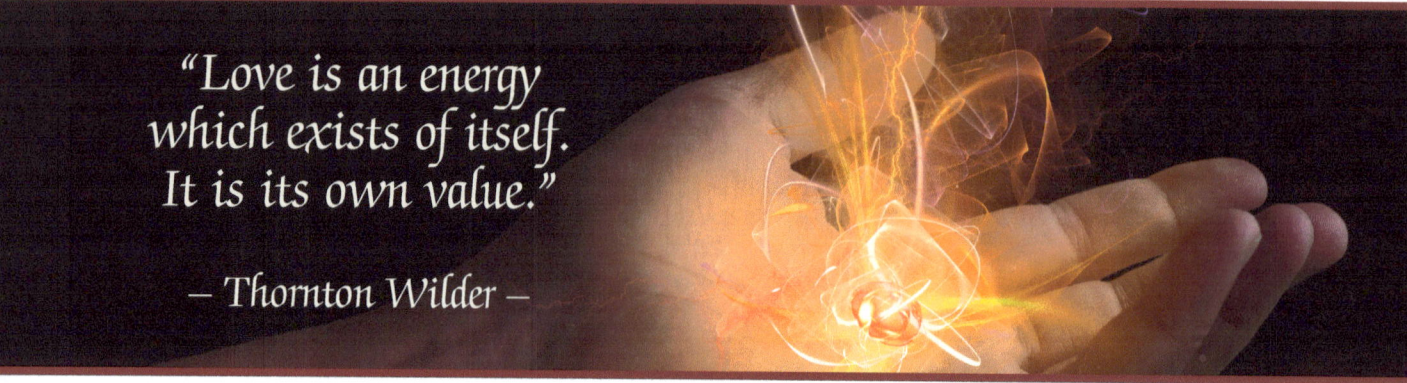

That last question is very important—perhaps the most important, actually. If you feel hesitancy because you're not sure if you really want to study energy work, that's different. But if you feel hesitant about a practitioner—whether you are studying with them or receiving energy work from them—step away. Why? Because you are energy.

Even if you haven't studied yet, if you get a feeling of hesitancy, that means you are experiencing something on an energetic level, and it's always best to heed the message, even if you don't understand it, yet. This would be akin to having a "gut feeling" about someone or something. Listen to your gut... and not just when you're hungry.

In some ways, when you study energy work with someone, you are agreeing to the energetic presence that they bring as well as the beliefs that they hold, even temporarily. So, it is your job and responsibility to really scratch beneath the surface and understand whether or not the practitioner is the right fit for you and where you are in your soul's evolution.

If someone is not the right fit today, they could be the right fit next year. What matters is that you listen to your intuition (which is a form of energy) while also doing your homework and researching everything.

In this world, there are many opportunities to learn how to work with energy—making even more reasons for you to do your due diligence. Unfortunately, just as there are wonderful practitioners, there are also charlatans.

"I wish that all of nature's magnificence, the emotion of the land, the living energy of place could be photographed."

– Annie Leibovitz –

Understanding How To Spot A Charlatan

Every industry seems to have charlatans these days. What is a charlatan? The simple answer is that it's like a cross between an impostor and a conman. They serve to con you out of your money, energy (many are "energy vampires"), and other resources, while they purport to be something they are not, often in the guise of wanting to help.

Today, there seem to be more charlatans at work every day. Unfortunately, when it comes to energy work, the world is rife with them, and most people who are just beginning to work with energy don't yet have the tools to discern who is real and who isn't. Of course, there are a few ways you can spot a charlatan when it comes to energy work, they include:

- **Aspirational Language** — If the promises seem too good to be true, they probably are. Ask more questions, read independent reviews (not testimonials), and check in on your own needs and emotions. If you are feeling desperate for a cure or some healing, you are more susceptible to charlatans who make big promises. Desperation gives off a vibe that makes you an attractive target.

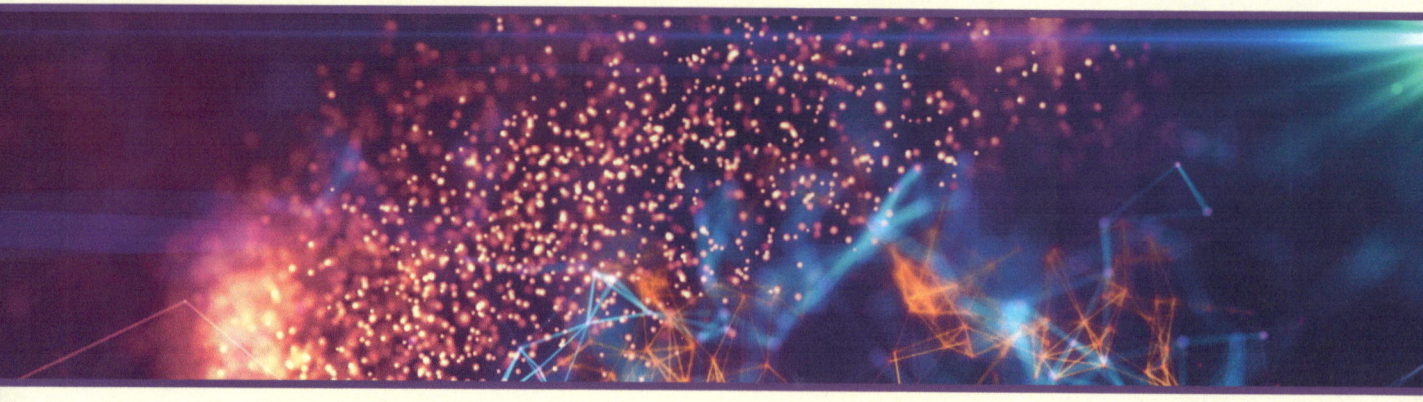

- **Minimal Requirement** – If the course of work can be achieved simply and quickly, it's probably not a course you want to take. (For example, full certification in a weekend is probably a warning sign, as most energy practices require a lot more study and practice. Additionally, certification online or virtually should also be a red flag, as introductory energy work requires in-person experience.)

One of the ways to think about it is this: Energy work involves impacting someone else's life. If the path to certification (or even a basic understanding) is too fast, what are you really learning? Energy work isn't benign. You aren't painting a wall that can be repainted; you are dealing with someone's life. The bar for entry, by design, should be higher than most. You wouldn't have surgery by someone who only took a weekend course over the internet, so please look at energy work in a similar way.

- **Fixed Thinking** – If the practitioner says their way is the "only" or "best" way, walk away. Yes, there is marketing, but there is also an inflated sense of self, belief in one's own skills, and role on this planet. When a practitioner has given themselves over to ego, it's usually a sign to step away. There will be somebody else you can learn from.

- **Urgency** – If the messaging to sign up has a level of urgency and crisis or danger attached to it, this is manipulative and is definitely not aligned with the universal premise behind energy work. Energy is a constant, therefore there is never any urgency to it. Manipulation is nuanced and can come in many forms—urgency is just one. If there is manipulative language, reconsider studying with this person. (Hint: This is also a good way to spot a scam in general, since a lot of them use urgency as a way to pressure people into signing up or joining whatever offer they're peddling.)

Charlatans are well-versed in the language of manipulation. They often create an unspoken need or fear, which then prompts an emotion in you, for which they (conveniently) offer a solution. Again, if you come to your search feeling desperate, you are an easy target for these types of people. If you come to your search feeling balanced, and the messaging sparks desperation or urgency in you, you also become a target.

The best way to find the right practitioner or practice is to do so when you are feeling rested, well-fed, hydrated, and balanced within yourself. You are more vulnerable to charlatans when you are feeling desperate, tired, overwhelmed, or overwrought. If you feel any of those things, it's time to engage in some self-care so that you can do your research from a better place.

At the end of the day, you can learn about energy work from many different people, in many different ways and places. What matters most is that you do your research and find a place to start that feels good in your body and soul... from your heart all the way down to your toes! When it feels good, it's probably a good fit.

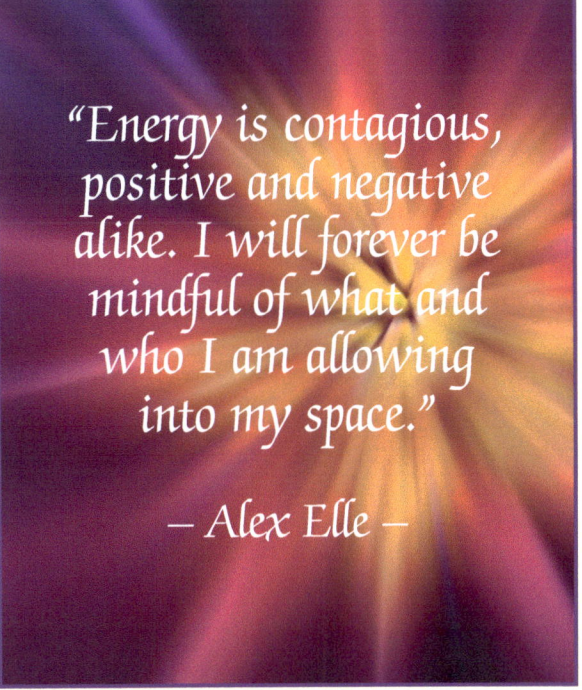

"Energy is contagious, positive and negative alike. I will forever be mindful of what and who I am allowing into my space."

— Alex Elle —

When the feeling changes, it's probably time to move on to a new teacher. Good teachers understand this and welcome it; they even encourage it. Conversely, the teacher that wants to keep you attached to them forever is probably the one you most need to step away from.

Why Do We Need To Understand Energy?

"What drains your spirit drains your body. What fuels your spirit fuels your body."

— Caroline Myss —

As the planet is evolving—as our species is evolving—we actually need to put an effort into understanding energy work a lot more today than we used to. Over centuries, especially the last century, we have abandoned a lot of the knowledge we once held as a collective. Of course, there are still many that hold this wisdom, but we are losing it at a rapid rate.

Think of the timeline for humanity. For thousands of years, knowing how to live with nature used to be part of our inherent understanding of life.

We used to know that the timing of nature served a purpose for our bodies and our minds.

We knew how to work in conjunction with seasons, weather, and wildlife, and this information was passed down from one generation to the next, almost effortlessly through story and practice.

Now, in the short span of just 100-200 years, we have gone away from most of the wisdom that we held for millennia as a human species.

It is important that we get back to understanding energy work because we are energy! We are not outside the system, we are in the system, part of the system, and we interact with the system on a daily basis. We have to understand it so that we can a) show up as our best selves in the system, and b) interact with the system appropriately. You can look around you, see anything that gives you a smile, and feel grateful. The possibilities are endless. We need to remember that everything we do has a ripple effect within the system, just as everything in the system has a ripple effect that touches us. So, it is very, very important for us to get back to a place where we understand that we are part of —not apart from—the system of energy, because we are energy ourselves.

Advancement and technology are great achievements, and in many ways, they have made life much easier on the planet for humans. But they are not the only way to live, nor should they be. The mistake most often made is assuming that it's an either/or choice. It's not. It's about both/and.

- We can practice energy work and engage in good uses of technology.
- We can understand our role in the larger system and still use our technological advances to offer surgeries that save lives.

It's never been about choosing one over the other; it's about learning how to incorporate both so that they complement each other and we can be better, overall.

When we understand energy work from this perspective, we set ourselves—and all of the planet—up for success. We can make decisions from a place of balance and consideration, rather than from a place of false expectations and urgency. Energy work is like those two or three puzzle pieces that fell under the sofa that have prevented us from completing the picture. When we dig them out from resting among the dust bunnies, clean them off, and put them in their proper place, we can finally see what's possible and have a clearer path forward.

How Do We Work Best With Energy Systems?

"The body's energy flow, like a river, must be kept clear to avoid stagnation and disease."

– Donna Eden –

Firstly, working with energy systems requires the due diligence we discussed previously. By conducting your research to know which protocol or method works best for you, you will be better able to truly engage with energy work when you begin. Being in alignment is an important piece of energy work, and since there are so many different practices available for study, knowing what will work best for you is the only way to begin.

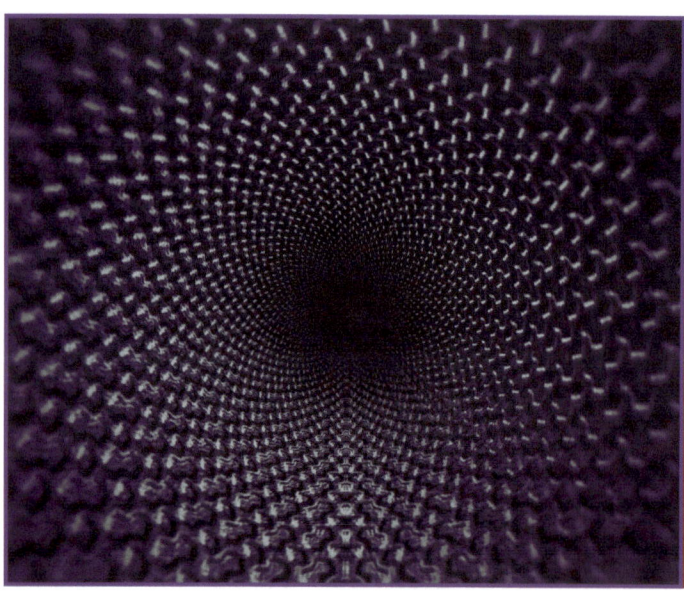

Beyond that, however, we also need to consider vibration and frequency. This is true both for what you want to study, as well as for working within the energy systems in the body, within nature, and on the planet. As everything is energy, it's only logical that there are different energetic systems that help to coordinate it all.

Let's start by breaking down "vibration" and "frequency" in easy to understand language.

Vibration vs. Frequency

The best way to explain the difference between vibration and frequency is by thinking of energy as a radio station. The radio station's signal is the vibration. It transmits at this specific number on the dial that people can tune into. Then, once you've tuned in, you control the frequency, which is like the volume knob. How high or low the vibration resonates is in part controlled by you and how you choose to interact with it. Each and every radio station (vibration) can be interacted with at both high and low volumes (frequencies). You control one aspect, and the energy systems control the other.

When you can identify both vibration and frequency, you can show up more consciously with more presence. This results in greater feelings of empowerment which then invites you to engage with the world on a much more holistic basis.

The question of how to work best with energy systems takes vibration and frequency into account. When you understand how to interact with the energy system and are mindful of its nuances, you can participate in it appropriately. As we are all energy, and all part of the energy systems of the planet, we are all participating in all the systems every day. The question of whether we are participating appropriately is what we need to focus on.

Think of a spider's web. One of the ways a spider knows it has trapped its next meal is because the web has vibrated from touch.

This is not enough, however. If a human touches a spider's web, the spider doesn't come running out with a bib under its chin, knife and fork at the ready.

The specific frequency of the vibration matters. The spider has learned which prey makes which frequency, and it knows when and how to act as a result.

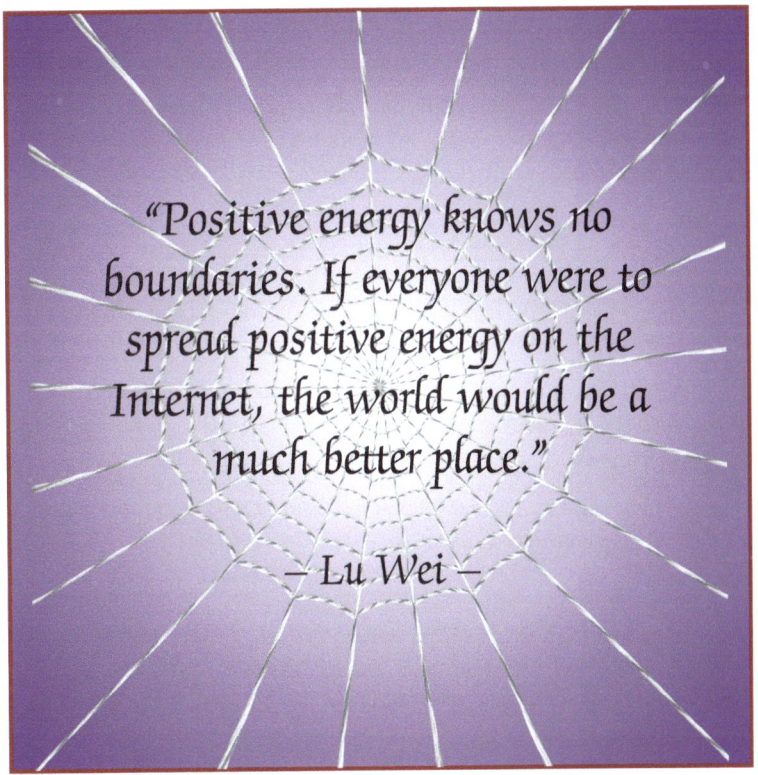

"Positive energy knows no boundaries. If everyone were to spread positive energy on the Internet, the world would be a much better place."

– Lu Wei –

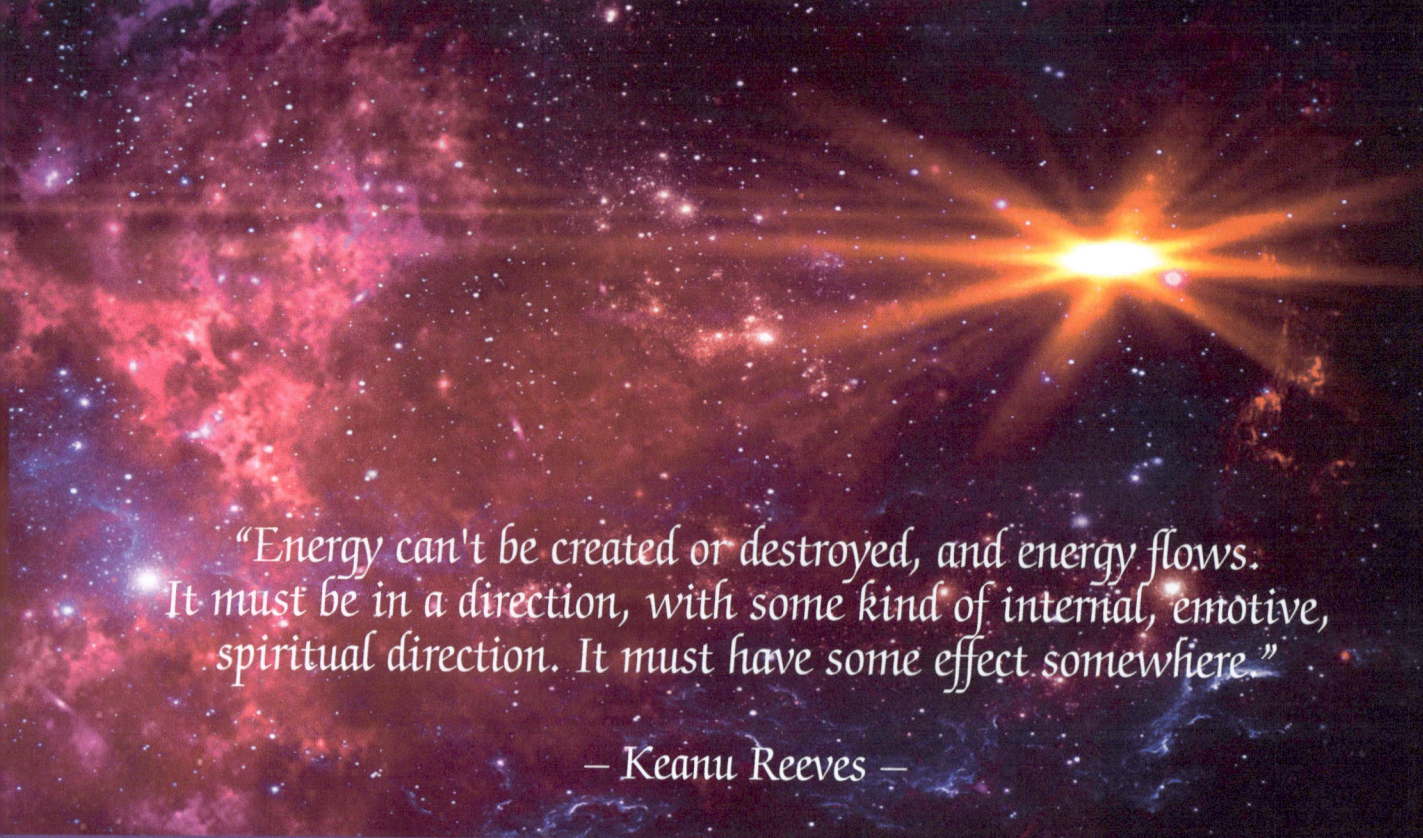

Now think of the energy systems of the planet as different strands in the web. Though each web is its own thing, they are all connected. A vibration on one strand will vibrate on all the other strands. When we touch the web—when we do something, consciously or not—we are affecting the whole web. Everything we do, no matter how small or big, in some way affects the whole.

We work best with all of the various energy systems when we remember this truth and take responsibility for our own energy—both the vibration and frequency at which we engage with life. While we can choose to stay within one or two energetic systems on the planet, we cannot forget that all of the systems are connected. For example, a wildlife conservationist might stay within the energy systems that are more nature-aligned. As a result, their own pace and focus might be different. If they were to stay there all the time, they would be completely incapacitated when they got on a plane or public transportation. Their personal system wouldn't be able to handle it if they didn't adjust to this different energy system.

When it comes to energy, being adaptable is just as important as understanding vibration and frequency so that you can adapt. It's also important to know when and how you can impact an energy system for the better. This is how we can work best with energy systems.

> *"Energy cannot be created or destroyed; it can only be changed from one form to another."*
>
> — Albert Einstein —

Now that we understand energy systems, it's also important to look at how energy can change within our own system, as well as what can impact our system and create change. Change is a constant and should always be expected on some level, so learning how to navigate change in relation to your own energy is important. But what creates change? Literally, anything.

Energy Change-Makers

Firstly, we need to differentiate between our environment and ourselves. That means that we have two types of stimulus that can create change: external and internal. External stimuli can be anything in your environment from the weather to someone's bad mood. Conversely, internal stimuli are usually less tangible, like chronic self-deprecating thoughts, constant emotional processing, or overconsumption of media. However, it can also be something more tangible and simple like getting a cold or the flu.

Regardless of whether the cause is internal or external, both will impact our energy in some way. Similarly, the stimulus can be both good and less-good. It's not just about being affected negatively, it can also be about being impacted positively by something.

For example, someone else's good mood at the result of a promotion at work can give us a boost of adrenaline and joy as we share in the happy energetic waves they are sending out. It can also follow that an hour or two later, we find ourselves crashing because of the removal of the same stimulus.

In short, anything and everything can affect and impact our energy, whether it's "good" or "bad" in essence. If you are alive and living in the world, your energy will be impacted by the world around you as well as how you process it. There is no way to escape this, nor should you want to. It's what makes you human and what makes life engaging. The goal, therefore, is to learn how to ride these waves with grace and ease by creating your own surfboard.

"There is a vitality, a life force, an energy, a quickening, that is translated through you into action, and because there is only one of you in all time, this expression is unique."

– Martha Graham –

Riding the Waves of Change

When change occurs within our own energy system, it can feel unsettling regardless of where it comes from—especially if we are used to having things be in balance. This type of shift requires some introspection followed by tools that can help us regain our footing. Most of the tools we would use can be filed under "self-care" and might include:

- Pampering (aromatherapy baths, facials, saunas, massage)

- Down time (meditation, naps, gentle walks in nature)

- Nourishment (healthy and/or comforting food and hydration)

- Reflection (reading, journaling, therapy, calling a friend)

Understanding what works best for you will help you create a shortlist that you can use at any time to redirect your energy and find balance. In addition to these self-care items, you can also keep a list of time-limited interventions that will buy you a little space and time until you can get to a self-care practice. In this instance, you would choose an item based on the amount of time you have. An example of this type of list can look like:

- **0-30 seconds:** *A few photos of your favorite people or pets*

- **30-60 seconds:** *A folder of favorite memes*

- **1-3 minutes:** *A compilation of quotes or a favorite comedian's video*

- **3+ minutes:** *A favorite song or a favorite video or compilation of videos*

Having tools at the ready can help you reset more easily when things around you have changed and you find your energy has gone a bit wonky. Being prepared makes it easier to redirect, as you don't have to think about what you should do, you just do it.

Since we can always expect change, creating these lists for yourself is a life-hack that can make everything easier.

"Thoughts are mental energy; they're the currency that you have to attract what you desire. Learn to stop spending that currency on thoughts you don't want."

– Wayne Dyer, PhD –

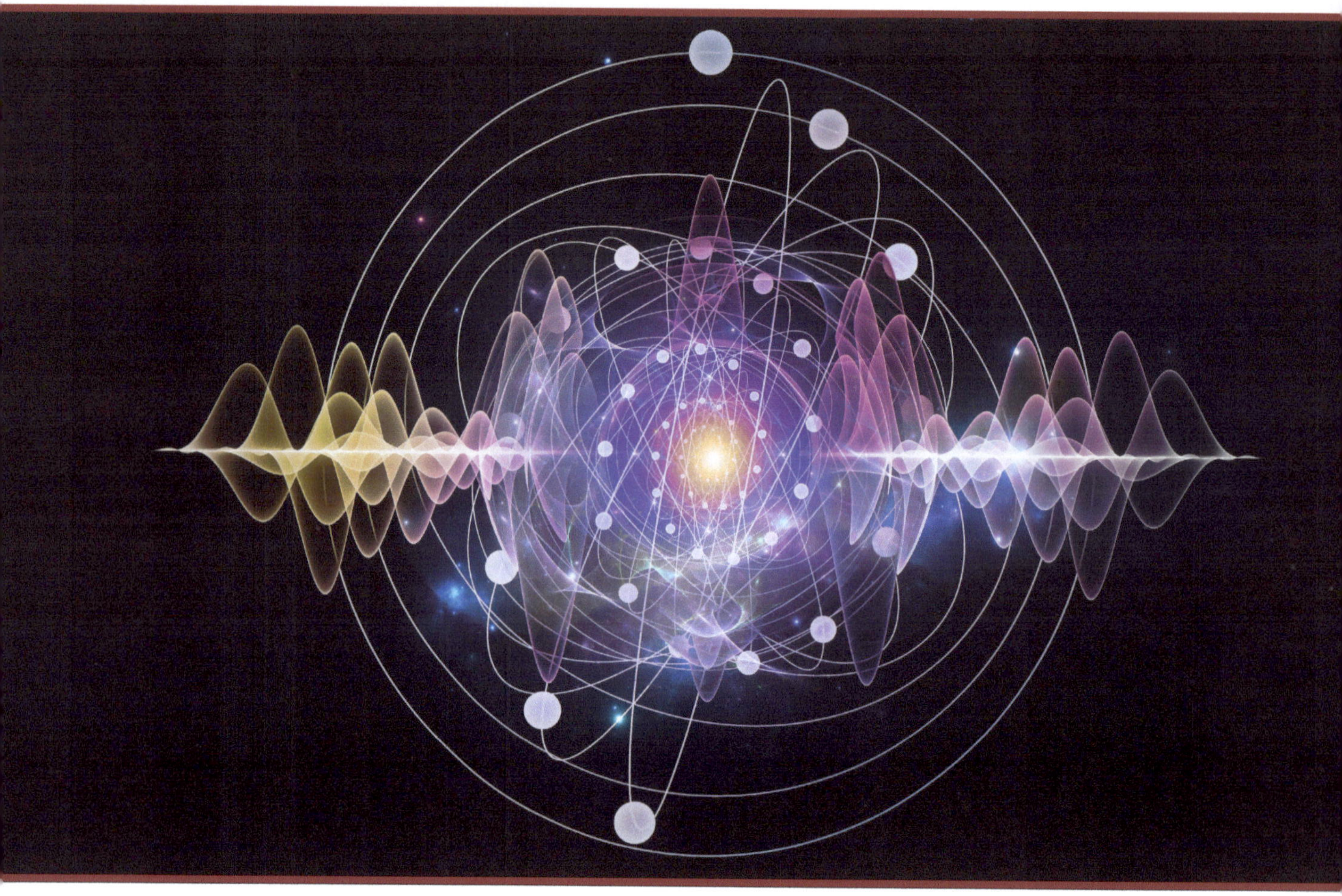

Minimizing Change from Internal Sources

Though both internal and external stimuli can create energetic changes for us, we can be proactive about minimizing the internal events that do this. External events will almost always be outside of our control, but how we react to them or engage with them is something we get to choose.

This means that we can invite ourselves to exercise a bit more influence over our own thoughts, behaviors, and emotions—or the things that make us human.

If, for example, you know that you get triggered when watching a specific show to the point that you feel deflated afterward, you might want to choose a different activity. (Yes, even if it's your roommate's favorite.)

Similarly, if you know that scrolling through social media in the morning invigorates you, but scrolling at night brings you down, changing your behavior can directly change the impact on your energy.

Even though both of these examples involve an external aspect, they originate from an internal decision: Where to put your attention.

When you start to raise your awareness to how your internal decisions affect your thoughts and emotions, you are reclaiming your energetic power.

Doomscrolling is only "doom-related" if it makes you feel bad and detached from yourself and the world around you.

Yes, there are times in our life when checking out can be good for us, but doing so on a regular basis is rarely a good idea. The key to all of this is understanding that it's a choice you get to make.

Just as it's a choice to reply to an angry text, an inconsiderate driver, or any other type of external event in your day, it's also a choice to react to your own internal events. The messaging you give yourself on a regular basis will always have a greater impact on your energy than anything internal.

As such, if you really want to ride energetic waves like a pro-surfer, you will want to start with yourself and check in on the type of energy you are bringing to your days through the thoughts you have and the language you use.

Once you've done that, you will really begin to understand how empowered you can be.

"Between stimulus and response, there is a space.

In that space is our power to choose our response. In our response lies our growth and our freedom."

— Victor Frankl —

Protecting Your Energy

"If you don't take responsibility for programming yourself, then someone else will."

– Paul McKenna –

Just as learning how to be flexible and adaptable to navigate change is important, you can also learn how to protect your energy. This section is not intended to be comprehensive, but instead to provide an overview of what's possible when it comes to energy work and creating protections. Each modality of study or tradition will have its own best practices and offer a deeper dive into the nuance of protection. Use the one that works for you.

That being said, there are certain aspects of protection that they all have in common, one of which is an understanding of what's ours—and what's not ours. This is the first step to incorporating any kind of energetic protection in your life. In fact, simply asking the question, "Is this mine?" is a good place to start.

"Is this mine?"

When it comes to energy, being able to discern what's yours and what's somebody else's allows you to address the situation with more clarity and choose a path forward that will be most helpful. For example, many empaths often report struggling when going into a hospital because of all the suffering going on.

As such, they are often taught to protect themselves before entering the building. This is not to disparage the patients in the hospital, rather it's to keep a firm boundary between what belongs to which person. If an empath is feeling the patient's suffering in a way that they are no longer able to help, that's not good for anybody.

Similarly, you often hear of protection being needed at large family gatherings, particularly over the holidays. This is not because people are inherently "bad" or "wrong" (though it sometimes can be), but it's often because in such groups there is a lack of respect for each other's emotional boundaries. This in turn can lead to energy violations that leave people feeling upset, angry, and/or depleted. It's such a common occurrence, actually, that it's usually incorporated in modern cultural narratives like movies and tv shows.

Protection, in this regard, is about both keeping energetic boundaries as well as physical ones. This can look like envisioning layers of energetic protection before ever entering the room and leaving a room before getting overwhelmed (excusing oneself to the bathroom always works).

Protecting your energy is first and foremost about connecting with yourself and knowing yourself well enough to make decisions that are in alignment with your best self. From there, you can implement a wide array of tools and exercises to move through life with more ease and less disruption.

"Inner peace begins the moment you choose not to allow another person or event to control your emotions."

— Pema Chödrön —

How Can You Use Energy?

"It takes as much energy to wish as it does to plan."

— Eleanor Roosevelt —

Energy is everything and everything is energy. This means that you can use it all the time, if you choose. Or you can use energy in ways that are more direct and specific. It's up to you.

How and when you use your knowledge of energy doesn't change the fact that it's always there. Always. In truth, however, developing an energy practice as well as an energy ethos is probably the best way to engage with energy on a regular basis.

What Is an Energy Ethos?

In this regard, an ethos is like a "guiding principle" for your life.

How you choose to work with energy will likely be grounded in your beliefs about it combined with your experience of it.

This will create a roadmap for you to engage with energy on a regular basis in a way that feels comfortable and allows you to grow and progress at your own pace.

Understanding your energy ethos, as well as what practices and traditions align with your ethos is an important step in your journey working with energy.

"Thought is pure energy, every thought you have, have ever had, and ever will have is creative. The energy of your thought never dies. It leaves your being and heads out into the universe, extending forever."

— Neale Donald Walsh —

In order to create your energy ethos, you will need to answer a couple questions:

- What do I want to experience with energy work and how do I want to feel about engaging with energy in a new way?

- How do I want my new experiences to impact my life going forward?

These questions will help guide you to creating a personal relationship with energy work that comes from within you. Once you have established that, you will be better able to connect with a practice, a tradition, and/or a teacher. Your energy ethos should be grounded in your core values as well as be in alignment with your life, or the life you want to create.

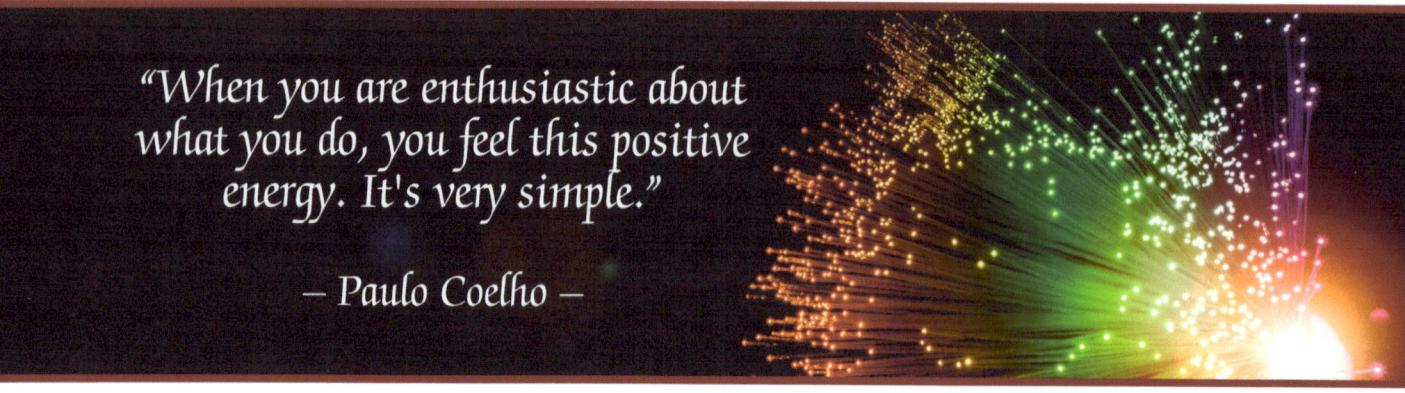

What Is an Energy Practice?

Most energy work traditions incorporate some aspect of practice. This means that when you begin to study energy work, you will need to practice. You will also benefit from a system of checks and balances that will help you hone your understanding and your skills. It's always best to learn from somebody who is further along the path, as they will have information and experience to impart that can help you.

Once you have identified a tradition or a teacher to study with, you will want to create a daily practice to help you connect with and understand energy on a personal level.

It's important to have a tangible personal understanding before ever moving into a professional capacity. Why? Because 1) it's a good parameter to have, and 2) it's common sense. If you don't know what it feels like and can't explain what it means to you, how can someone ever trust you to help them? More importantly, though, why should they?

There's a saying among helping professionals that feels apt here: Someone can only take you as far as they, themselves, have gone. If they don't know the landscape, they will struggle to walk you through it.

So, you should hold the same level of understanding for yourself, even if you don't want to become a professional energy worker and just want to learn about energy for personal use and growth.

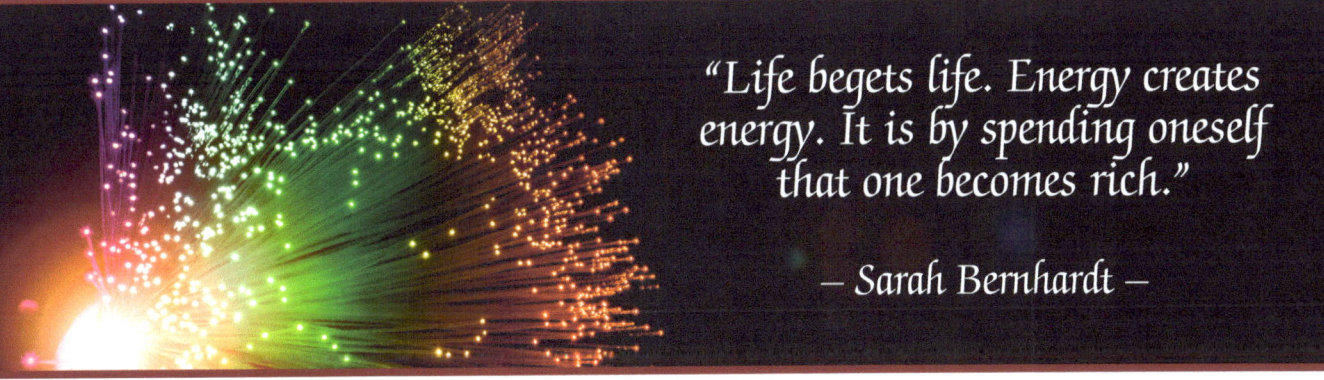

"Life begets life. Energy creates energy. It is by spending oneself that one becomes rich."

— Sarah Bernhardt —

To create a daily practice, the sky's the limit! Your practice can (and should) look like whatever will work best for you, and it can include things like:

- Meditation (guided, structured, or free)

- Movement (yoga, tai chi, forest bathing)

- Nourishment (diet can impact energy)

- Art (expressing oneself is a way to connect with energy)

- Tools (Tarot, runes, card decks, etc)

- Free-flow writing

- Specific practices based on the tradition you study

Working with energy is a gift you give to yourself, and then bring to the world. When you begin to understand the basics of how energy works—and accept that everything is energy—you can truly start to live from a different place. Not only do you feel more empowered, but from an empowered state you often take more responsibility for your own life which allows you to be more deliberate about creating a life that fulfills you.

This, in some ways, is the most wonderful side effect of understanding energy: A more fulfilled life. What a gift!

Conclusion

Whether you want to learn about energy to use it professionally or to simply create a better life for yourself and your family, the choice is yours. Ultimately, both will be of benefit to the world. More people working with energy, from a place of truly understanding what it is, can only bring about greater planetary change, for the better. Though energy work can be (and has been) misused by a small number of people over millennia, it also holds the promise of a more beneficial future. This is because understanding energy is about understanding ourselves—who we are and who we can be.

When you understand that everything is energy, and that energy is either dormant or active, you unlock the door to living a more deliberate life. The key is accepting that working with energy creates empowerment, and empowerment creates possibility. From there, probability is the next logical step... and it all starts with you!

Working with energy is something you can learn at any age, anywhere, and create something new in your life. It changes how you interact with the world around you, usually for the better. When you understand energy, your world opens up and becomes so much bigger than anything you have experienced before. Simultaneously, it also becomes much more connected, which makes it feel somehow smaller, in the best possible ways.

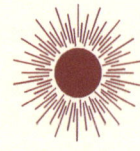 *"The more you lose yourself in something bigger than yourself, the more energy you will have."*

— Norman Vincent Peale —

"The quality of your life is based on the choices you make."

— Martina E. Faulkner —

About the Author

Martina E. Faulkner is a cross-genre author whose work focuses primarily on exploring what it means to be human, both the unique and the universal. She holds a trifecta in the mental health/healing world as a therapist, certified life coach, and Reiki Master Teacher. This distinctive background allows her to draw on her professional and personal experience in her writing, whether fiction, nonfiction, or poetry.

A self-proclaimed Anglophile, Martina drinks tea daily, loves walks in nature, and enjoys looking at beautiful images from the British Isles while dreaming up her next book. You can read her regular column ('Unique and Universal') on Substack, follow her on Instagram and Facebook @martinaefaulkner, or visit martinaefaulkner.com.

As a children's author, Martina's debut children's book, <u>When the World Went Quiet</u>, was given as a gift to Sir David Attenborough, who referred to it as "charming."

Other Books

Understanding Resilience
Understanding Gratitude
Understanding Grief
Understanding Karma
50 and F*ck It!
What if..?
Love and Pain
Infinite In My Heart
Me: 365
The Author's Journey
Crafting the Perfect College Essay

Children's Books

When the World Went Quiet
Princess Wigglebottom and the Forgotten Christmas

www.ingramcontent.com/pod-product-compliance
Lightning Source LLC
Chambersburg PA
CBHW041440120626
46547CB00002B/278